AN INSTANT GUIDE TO

BUTTERFLIES

The most familiar species of
North American butterflies
described and illustrated in color

Pamela Forey and Cecilia Fitzsimons

BONANZA BOOKS
New York

First published 1987 by Bonanza Books,
distributed by Crown Publishers, Inc.

© 1987 Atlantis Publications Ltd.

Printed in Spain

ISBN 0–517–61801–X

CONTENTS

Introduction

This is a book for those who want to be able to identify the butterflies that they see on the roadsides, on a camping trip or in their backyards. Many people who do not have the time or opportunity to make a close study of them would still appreciate some means of easily identifying a butterfly that catches their eye along a forest trail in a National Park, in the yard or even on a vacant lot.

We have selected from several hundred North American butterflies those species most likely to be encountered in the open countryside of the more heavily populated areas of the United States and Canada, as well as those likely to be seen along streets or in parks and gardens. Emphasis has been given to the butterflies of the temperate areas of North America; and the tropical species that occur in the southern states have, on the whole, been excluded. Exceptions have been made for those southern butterflies that migrate northwards in large numbers each year, to become common throughout the continent in the summer months.

How to use this book

We have divided the book into sections on the basis of color, to make it as easy as possible for you to find your butterfly quickly. Since butterflies are so variable in their coloration and exhibit so many color combinations, we have created twelve different color sections to cover all the possibilities. These sections are: **Purple and Yellow; Yellow; Orange or Orange & Black; Brown & Orange; Brown or Gray-brown; Brown with Eyespots; Brown & Green; Black with Red, Yellow or White Stripes; Black & Blue; Blue; Gray or Gray-blue; White.**

It is not always easy to determine whether a butterfly is, for instance, dark brown and orange or black and orange. In such an event, if you have decided that your butterfly is brown and orange but you cannot find it in that section, then check in the black and orange section (or even in the blue section, since many female blues are brown and orange, see page 9), to see if it has been included there.

Guide to identification

First decide to which color section your butterfly belongs. Page numbers given at the end of each description will enable you to turn directly to the relevant section.

Purple & Yellow: Only one butterfly, the Mourning Cloak. **14**

Yellow: Usually easy to distinguish but the Orange Sulphur may appear more orange than yellow sometimes. **15–19, 113**

Orange or Orange & Black: Many butterflies have this combination of colors on their wings, often with complicated patterns. They may be confused with the butterflies in the following section which may have such dark brown wings that it is difficult to decide whether the color is black or brown. **20–37, 114, 115**

Brown & Orange: Many butterflies have this combination of colors on their wings; they may be nearly all brown with a few orange spots or have more equal patterns of brown and orange. Many female blues have brown and orange wings and these have been included in the Blue section. If you cannot find your butterfly in this section, then check in Blues and in the Orange or Orange & Black section. **38–55, 116**

Brown or Gray-brown: Many butterflies have more or less dull brown or gray-brown wings. They may be plain brown, or have darker markings or whitish spots. **56–73, 117**

Brown with Eyespots: These butterflies have distinctive eyespots on their wings. However, the final two butterflies in the previous section may sometimes have small eyespots on their wings and should be checked also. **74–79**

Brown & Green: The green color makes these butterflies easy to distinguish from others. **80–81**

Black with Red, Yellow or White stripes: A variety of butterflies, usually large and many with spectacular patterns on their wings. The stripes are often made of many separate blotches. **82–91, 118**

Black & Blue: These butterflies have black wings, suffused with a varying amount of blue. Two of the butterflies in the previous section have blue forms which mimic the blue and black Pipe Vine Swallowtail butterfly in this section. **84, 92–93**

Blue: Male blue butterflies and some hairstreaks have blue wings, females have browner wings, often with a covering of blue scales. Some species have orange spots around the borders. **94–101, 119–121**

Gray or Gray-blue: A few butterflies have steel-colored wings or gray wings checkered with white. **102–105**

White: Easy to distinguish from other butterflies, with white wings, often with black veins and markings. Some have orange wing tips or yellowish marbling on the wings. **106–112**

Making a positive identification

In the box at the top of each page you will find the name of the butterfly and two other pieces of information, the size of the butterfly (given in the size symbol and as an actual measurement from wing tip to wing tip, see Fig. 1) and the time of year at which it is likely to be seen. Latitude and elevation are critical factors influencing the emergence of butterflies from their pupae, and where a species flies at different times in the northern and southern parts of its range, this has been indicated. Where a butterfly flies in both mountain and lowland areas it usually emerges earlier in the season in the lowlands than in the mountains.

Fig. 1 Key to size symbols

 Less than 1¼ inches

 1¼–2¾ inches

 2¾–4 inches

 4–5½ inches

On each page, four boxes of text provide details which make positive identification possible. The first box gives information on color and wing patterns which, together with the illustration, enable you to identify your butterfly. The second box gives you information on the caterpillar and its foodplant. Details of habitat and biology are given in the third box. Finally the fourth box indicates some species with which it might be confused and/or includes a description of the group to which it belongs.

Characteristic features

Included here are the details of color and wing pattern, on both sides of the wings, that are characteristic of this species. Where wing shape or details of stance are important these are also indicated.

The caterpillar and its foodplants

The second box provides a description of the caterpillar and its foodplants. The foodplant is often one of the most likely places to find adult butterflies or at least the females. The males may be elsewhere.

Biology, habitat and distribution of the butterfly

Details of the habitats in which a butterfly is likely to be found are given in the third box. Details of biology which may also aid identification, like flight and perching behavior, mud puddling and feeding habits, nectar plants etc., are also given here.

Because of the wide variation in the climate and geography of North America, the area and habitat in which a butterfly may be found are important clues to its identity. Many of the butterflies found in this book fall into four groups, those found east of the Rocky Mountains; those found west of the Rocky Mountains; those found in the more tropical areas of the south, migrating north in summer; and those found in the far north, spreading south in the mountains. The distribution of the species is given in the map in the illustration below (Fig. 2).

Similar species
Finally in the fourth box are given some of the butterflies with which this one might be confused. Those species printed in **bold** type are illustrated, either as featured species or in the Other Common Species sections; those printed in ordinary type are not. Not all related or similar species have been mentioned since there are several hundred butterflies in North America. Those omitted altogether are much less likely to be seen, either because they are local or rare or because they live in inaccessible habitats like swamps or on mountain tops.

Other common species
At the end of the book you will find pages of other common species. These are mostly less widespread than the featured butterflies or less likely to be encountered. However, some of them, like some skippers and fritillaries, are common butterflies which have not been included in the main part of the book because they are similar to species already featured.

Now you are ready to use this book. It is designed to fit into your pocket, so take it with you on your next trip and don't forget to check your sightings on the check-list provided with the index. Butterflies are amongst the most beautiful of the living things in North America, far more beautiful alive and in flight than in a box. Many are endangered by land development like other animal and plant species and some are protected by Federal or State law. So please do not collect them but take a photograph instead.

Fig. 2 Distribution map

● Widespread and resident in this area

○ Partial distribution only or reaching the limits of its distribution in this area

✴ Migrates into this area during the summer

Life history of a butterfly

Butterflies, like many other insects, have a complicated life cycle. After mating, adult female butterflies lay their eggs on a wide variety of plants, sometimes singly, sometimes in rows or clusters, usually on the undersides of leaves.

The larvae or caterpillars emerge after a few days or may remain in the eggs over the winter to emerge in spring. The caterpillar, as illustrated in the diagram opposite, is quite different to the adult butterfly in form and lifestyle. At first the caterpillar is very small but it grows quickly, feeding on the leaves or flowers of the foodplant on which the eggs were laid. It sheds its skin several times during this period and its appearance may change considerably after each skin change. The description given in the texts refers to the fully grown caterpillar.

Fig. 3 Specimen Page

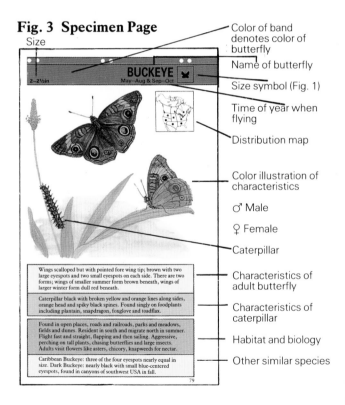

Size

Color of band denotes color of butterfly

BUCKEYE
2–2½in
May–Aug & Sep–Oct

Name of butterfly

Size symbol (Fig. 1)

Time of year when flying

Distribution map

Color illustration of characteristics

♂ Male

♀ Female

Caterpillar

Wings scalloped but with pointed fore wing tip; brown with two large eyespots and two small eyespots on each side. There are two forms; wings of smaller summer form brown beneath, wings of larger winter form dull red beneath.

Characteristics of adult butterfly

Caterpillar black with broken yellow and orange lines along sides, orange head and spiky black spines. Found singly on foodplants including plantain, snapdragon, foxglove and toadflax.

Characteristics of caterpillar

Found in open places, roads and railroads, parks and meadows, fields and dunes. Resident in south and migrate north in summer. Flight fast and straight, flapping and then sailing. Aggressive, perching on tall plants, chasing butterflies and large insects. Adults visit flowers like asters, chicory, knapweeds for nectar.

Habitat and biology

Caribbean Buckeye: three of the four eyespots nearly equal in size. Dark Buckeye: nearly black with small blue-centered eyespots, found in canyons of southwest USA in fall.

Other similar species

79

12

Once it reaches its full size it becomes lethargic. At this stage many caterpillars spin a cocoon of silk, but all find a hiding place unique to the species, and shed their skin for a final time. The form that emerges is quite different (see diagram) and is called a pupa or chrysalis. Its skin soon hardens, and inside radical changes take place in the form of the animal, a process called metamorphosis. At the end of this process the pupa splits open and the adult butterfly emerges.

The adult butterfly has a "furry" body divided into three parts, the head, thorax and abdomen. Attached to the thorax are two pairs of brightly colored, scale-covered wings (two fore wings and two hind wings), and three pairs of legs. In its mouth the butterfly has a long, coiled, tubular proboscis which it uses to feed on the nectar of flowers; there are furry palps in front of the proboscis and long clubbed antennae on the top of the head.

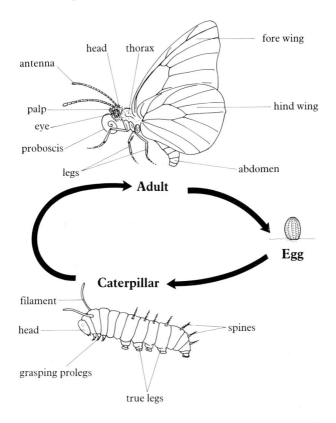

13

Wings dark purple-brown with a row of bright blue spots near the edges and ragged yellow margins. Underside mottled gray with yellowish border.

Caterpillar black with red and white spots; it has many spines and bristles. Larvae feed together in silk web at first, later in groups or alone, on willows, elms, aspen and poplar.

Found in woodland clearings, along river beds, in parks and gardens. Flight straight, alternately sailing and flapping. Usually bask with wings open in the afternoon, or in shade with wings closed when hot. Adults feed on sap flows especially on oak trees, and fermenting fruit; occasionally on flower nectar.

No similar butterfly.

Smallest yellow. Wings yellow with black wing tips and broad black bands along rear of fore wing and front of hind wing. Female may also have black borders. Undersides have olive scales.

Caterpillar dark green with purple stripe on the back and black and yellow side stripes. Feeds on members of the daisy family, including sneezeweeds, fetid and cultivated marigolds.

Found in dry open areas like old fields, hillsides, coastal areas, prairies and deserts of southwest, canyons, roadsides and railroads. Resident in southern USA and migrate north in summer. Often move along roads and rivers using composite weeds for caterpillars. Flight erratic, just above the ground.

Fairy Yellow: no black bar on hind wing, no olive scales beneath.

15

Small butterfly, with bright yellow wings and brown or black wing tips and margins, wider on males. Border has scalloped inside edge. Underside of hind wings has reddish spot near upper margin.

Caterpillar green and downy with white lines on side. Feeds on legumes including senna, clovers and partridge pea.

Found in open areas like sandy fields, roadsides and railroad tracks. Resident in southern USA and migrate north in large numbers in spring and summer. Males gather at mud puddles or patrol during day. Flight a zigzag close to ground and can fly in high winds. Feed at flowers like asters and goldenrods.

Fairy Yellow: southeastern species, hind wing underside brown in winter, white in summer; fore wing of male has black bar.
Dwarf Yellow: broad black bands on wings.

Wings clear yellow with black borders, often tinged white in female. There are single spots on both fore and hind wings, black on fore wing, black with red rim on hind wing. Underside of hind wing has row of brown spots around margin.

Caterpillar bright green with white lines on the sides and a dark line on the back. Feeds on legumes, usually white clovers, as well as other clovers and trefoils.

Found in open spaces, especially meadows rich in clover, parks and suburbs, often fluttering in large numbers on sunny days. They settle, especially on yellowed leaves, if the sun goes in. Males gather at mud puddles on roads and by streams to drink. Adults visit many flowers, especially yellow ones.

Orange Sulphur: wings orange or orange-tinged but often difficult to distinguish these two butterflies. Other sulphurs lack the row of brown spots on underside of hind wing.

CLOUDLESS GIANT SULPHUR
(S) all year; (N) summer—fall

2–2¾in

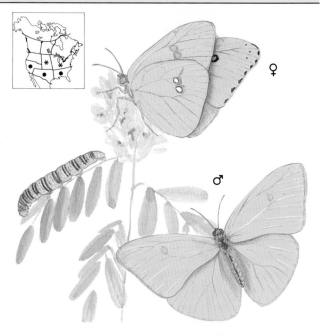

♀

♂

Wings of males clear yellow; of females yellow or white, with black spots on wing margins and with a black spot in center of fore wing. Underside of each hind wing of both sexes has a pair of silvery spots.

Caterpillar yellow or green with rows of small black tubercles. Feeds on legumes, including sennas and clovers, by night and hides by day in tent formed of silk and leaves.

Found in open spaces including beaches, disturbed ground, open brush, abandoned fields and roads. Resident in southern states and migrate north in summer in the east and midwest. Flight strong and direct. Males gather at mud puddles and both sexes visit flowers like bougainvillea, morning glories and lantana.

Most other yellow sulphurs much smaller, with black or colored borders to the wings or without the spot on the underside of the hind wings.

Wings yellow suffused with orange and often tinged with pink; with black borders. Single black spot on fore wing, reddish spot on hind wing. Underside of hind wing has a row of brown spots.

Caterpillar dark green with white lines on the sides. Feeds on legumes including white clover and alfalfa. May become a pest in alfalfa fields.

Found in open spaces, especially alfalfa fields and clover-rich meadows, suburbs and parks, where large males often fly high and fast. Smaller males behave more like Yellow Sulphurs and join them at mud puddles. Adults visit wide variety of flowers like dandelions, red clovers and milkweeds.

Common Sulphur: no orange on wings. Other sulphurs: no row of brown spots on underside of hind wing, many lack black borders.

19

Wings bright orange, with broad black border on both wings in male but on fore wing and top of hind wing only in female. Single black spot on fore wing. Underside of hind wings mottled but without spots.

Caterpillar slender, green and downy with a black, yellow and white side stripe. Feeds on legumes including sennas and partridge pea.

Found in open areas including old fields in east and desert scrub in west, also open woodland edges, pine woods, roadsides and meadows. Resident in south and migrates north in summer in large numbers. Males gather at mud puddles, rarely visit flowers. Flight an erratic zigzag if disturbed.

Orange Sulphur: underside of hind wings has spots in center and on the margins.

Wings of male bright orange, of female paler orange; undersides of wings mottled purple-brown or gray. Fore wings are hooked at apex, hind wings have narrow tails. Fall and spring forms brighter than summer form with more pointed hook on fore wings.

Caterpillar gray-green with many minute warts and narrow at posterior end. Has small orange horns on head. Feeds on goatweed; older caterpillars live in folded leaves of plant.

Found in old fields, woodland edges, on country roads and farmyards in the great plains. Flight fast and erratic, then settles with folded wings so that the orange butterfly "disappears" to look like a brown leaf. Adults feed on rotting fruit, sap and manure; they hibernate in winter.

Tropical Leafwing: wings scalloped in outline, not smooth as in Goatweed Butterfly, found in southern Texas.

21

QUESTION MARK
May–Jun & Aug–Sep

2½in

Two forms, summer and fall. Wings blue-bordered; orange-red spotted with black, and brown undersides in fall form. Summer form has dark hind wings and violet undersides. Silver "comma and dot," forming "question mark" on underside of hind wing.

Caterpillar rust-colored with many branched black or reddish spines and longitudinal red or yellow lines. Young larvae feed in groups, older ones alone on elm, hackberry, nettles and hops.

Found in woodland clearings and edges, wooded roads and meadows. Adults hibernate in winter or migrate south, emerging in April or May. Flight fast and erratic. Males perch on tree branches, chasing other males or large insects. Adults feed on rotting fruit and sap, bask in the afternoon sun with wings open.

Comma: underside of wing bears "comma" instead of "question mark." Other anglewing and comma butterflies are very similar, distinguished by differences in size and markings.

Two forms, summer and fall. Wings orange in fall form, with dark margins and underside patterned in brown. Summer form has dark hind wings with golden brown undersides. Both have a silver "comma" mark on the underside of the hind wing.

Caterpillar light green to brown with darker blotches and many branched spines. Foodplants include nettles, false nettles, elms and hops. May be a pest on hops.

Found in woodland clearings and edges, in river valleys and open disturbed ground. An aggressive butterfly with fast and erratic flight. Males perch in afternoon, often on bare wood, flying out at passing insects or to intercept females. Adults feed on rotting fruit, tree sap and carrion. Hibernate in winter.

Question Mark: wings blue-bordered, underside bears "question mark" instead of "comma." Satyr Anglewing: wings golden, not orange and without dark border; mainly western species.

Wings brilliant orange-red with black veins and spots. There are three white black-rimmed spots near the front of each fore wing. Underside of fore wing orange, of hind wing brown with bright silver spots and streaks.

Caterpillar dark gray with longitudinal orange stripes and six rows of branched black spines. Feeds on passion flower vines.

Found in open sunny meadows, fields and pastures, also in suburban back yards, wherever there are many flowers. Resident in south and migrates north in summer. Fast-flying butterflies. Males patrol in search of females. Adults visit flowers avidly in search of nectar, especially lantana and shepherd's needle.

Small fritillaries have no silver spots on underside. Large fritillaries, although silver-spotted below, have rounded wings and extensive black spotting on upper surface.

Wings orange with complex zigzag lines and spots but no spots on wings near bases. Underside of hind wing has silver spots on base, a wide yellow band and a row of silver triangles near the brown margin. Female is darker, especially in wing base area.

Caterpillar velvety black with black orange-based spines. Eggs laid in late summer and fall, on or near their foodplants which are violets. Caterpillars do not begin to feed until spring.

Found in open areas, particularly in moist meadows and open areas of damp woods. More common in east than west and absent from extreme south. Flight strong and fast, males patrol regularly, stopping to sip nectar at flowers like milkweeds and thistles. Females most obvious in late summer when laying eggs.

There are many similar large fritillaries, including **Aphrodite**: has similar range, however has one black spot near base of fore wing and narrow yellow band on underside of hind wing.

25

Fore wing truncated. Wings orange with heavy zigzag black lines, black veins and spots; there is no black margin. Underside of hind wing patterned in brown with whitish patch near base, and gray-violet in color on outer half.

Caterpillar purple-black with a velvety black band along the sides and many branched brown spines on yellowish tubercles. Feeds by night on violets and hides during the day.

Found in wet meadows, hay fields and pastures especially near woodland or streams, in mountains in the south and more common in the east than in the west. Flight low and jerky, males patrol meadows when sunny, stopping to sip nectar at flowers like black-eyed susans and ox-eye daisies, or mint and dogbane.

Other small fritillaries, like Western Meadow Fritillary, have rounded fore wings. Silver-bordered Fritillary is a small fritillary with silver spots on underside of hind wing.

Fore wings bright orange copper in color, with black spots and black margin. Hind wings gray-black with irregular orange patch on rear margin.

Caterpillar "short and fat," green with pink markings and covered with short hairs. It feeds on the undersides of leaves of sheep sorrel or sometimes on curly dock.

Found in disturbed ground, vacant lots, old fields and roadsides, where the weeds which are its caterpillar host plants grow, in mountains in southern part of its range. Males perch on tall daisies or other plants and fly out at insects. Adults visit buttercups, clovers, ox-eye daisies and butterflyweed.

No other North American butterfly has the bright orange-copper fore wings and bicolored hind wings. Other coppers with similar wing patterns have browner wings, like **Bronze Copper**.

Wings broad, black with large orange spots, so that about half the area of the fore wings is orange. Underside of hind wings orange with white spots. Body large, rounded and hairy. Basks with wings partly open.

Caterpillar blue-green or cream in color, with a darker stripe on the back and a pale yellow stripe on each side. Feeds on grasses.

Found in trails and glades of forests, northern meadows, streamsides and bogs. Males perch on grasses in forest clearings, patrolling occasionally before returning to their perch. Flight relatively weak and slow, for a skipper, and close to the ground. Adults visit flowers for nectar.

No other skippers have the distinctive large orange spots on the black wings.

Black fore wings suffused in center with orange. Hind wings orange with black border. Underside of fore wings black and orange, of hind wings orange. Antenna ends in blunt club. Basks with fore wings raised, hind wings flat.

Caterpillar grass green with a brown head. Feeds on various grasses, including millet and cultivated rice.

Found in wet meadows amongst tall grasses, or on borders of slow streams or marshes; later in summer more widely found in pastures and old fields. Flies low, with skipping flight among the grasses, hiding in them if disturbed. Visits many small plants for nectar, including wood sorrel and pickerel weed.

Small size and bicolored wings are distinctive. Most other skippers have hooked antennae. Many other male skippers have a black sex-brand on each fore wing.

Wings have broad crescent of orange, broken by black lines and with a black margin. Black markings are heavier on female. Underside of fore wing has unmarked base, of hind wing creamy yellow, with brown lines and a light crescent on the margin.

Caterpillar dark brown with broken yellow bands and eight rows of brown tubercles. Feed in groups on asters, especially on New England asters, leaving skeletons of leaves, but spin no web.

Found in meadows, on roadsides, vacant lots and other open areas. Males patrol open areas or perch on ground, flying at other butterflies and insects. They may be seen drinking at mud puddles. Flight alternately flapping and gliding. Adults visit wide variety of flowers like dogbane and milkweeds.

Other crescents have markings on underside of base of fore wing. Field Crescent and **Mylitta Crescent** are both western species, the first flying at higher elevations than the second.

Wings with crescent of orange across both wings, black margins and black blotches near wing bases. Underside of hind wing has marginal row of silver and brown blotches; underside of fore wing orange and brown.

Caterpillar dark brown with yellow spots, a broken yellow stripe along each side and many brown spines. Feed in groups on asters, sunflowers and wingstem, reducing leaves to skeletons.

Found near streams and rivers, in open woodland and wet meadows, often in areas with sandy soil. It flies slowly, flapping and gliding low over the ground; males perch and patrol open areas in the afternoon or may drink at mud puddles. Adults sip nectar from clovers, milkweeds and coneflowers.

Similar butterflies are found in north and west. **Northern Checkerspot**, Harris' Checkerspot and Gorgone Crescent (a prairie species) distinguished by details on undersides of wings.

31

Jun–Aug

1½–2½in

Wings black with orange spots near wing bases, several rows of white spots and a row of touching orange spots on the margin. Undersides of wings with similar pattern.

Caterpillar orange with black transverse stripes and seven rows of branched black spines. They feed in groups in silk webs on their foodplants, turtleheads or false foxgloves.

Found in damp meadows or marshes, on or very near to their caterpillar foodplants but Ozark butterflies are found on drier, often wooded, hillsides. Flight slow and near the ground; males perch on shrubs near the ground. They feed on clover and milkweed nectar. These butterflies are distasteful to birds.

Chalcedon, Edith's Checkerspot, and Anicia Checkerspot are very variable and may resemble the Baltimore but all have bands of yellow or orange spots across the insides of the wings.

This butterfly mimics the Monarch and Queen butterflies. It has orange-brown wings, with black veins and black white-spotted borders. One black transverse vein curves across the hind wings. Undersides similar in color and pattern.

Caterpillar olive green with a white blotch and white sides, mimics a bird dropping. Fore end is humped and it has two bristles behind head. Foodplants mostly willows and poplar.

Found in wet meadows and marshland with low-growing vegetation or on land adjacent to such areas, near rivers and ponds. Males perch on the ground or on low plants and patrol with a slow flapping and sailing flight. Adults feed on carrion early in year, on flower nectar later.

Monarch and **Queen** have no transverse vein on hind wings.

33

Wings orange, with wide black margins spotted with white, and black veins. It has long fore wings. Undersides of wings similar in pattern but paler in color. Distasteful to birds since they contain poisons from milkweeds.

Caterpillar transversely striped in white, yellow and black, with a pair of filaments at the head and rear. Feeds on poisonous milkweeds. Poisons retained by adults.

Spend winter in Mexico, southern Calif., sometimes in Florida, in large clusters in eucalyptus and pine groves. Migrate north in spring; found wherever milkweeds grow, from mountains to cities, reaching much of N. America by fall. Fall butterflies congregate and migrate south. Flight slow and soaring.

Viceroy mimics the Monarch and gains protection from birds in so doing; it is smaller and has a transverse black line across the hind wings.

Wings red-brown with wide black margins and fine black veins; it has white spots on the long fore wings. Undersides similar but browner and with heavier veins. Distasteful to birds due to poisons from milkweeds.

Caterpillar transversely striped in dark brown and white with yellow spots and three pairs of filaments. Feeds on poisonous milkweeds, and poisons are retained by adults.

Found in open places, prairies, deserts, and river valleys, at higher elevations in dry seasons. Queens do not migrate north like Monarchs but spread as far as Kansas in summer. Males patrol during the day in search of females. Flight slow and soaring. Adults take nectar from milkweeds.

In southern USA **Viceroy** mimics the more common Queen rather than the **Monarch**. It can be distinguished by the transverse black line on the hind wing.

Wings reddish-orange with black tips with a few white spots; two blue spots near rear edge of hind wing. Underside of wings patterned in olive and white with large pink area on fore wing and two large blue eyespots on hind wing.

Caterpillar black, cross-banded with yellow and with row of white spots along the side, and black spines. Feeds mostly on cudweed, pussytoes and related plants, making nest near top.

Found in grassland, river beds and canyons, also in gardens; commoner in east than in west. Males drink at wet spots on dirt trails. May be seen in the afternoon on bare ground on the lee side of hills or on low vegetation with wings open. Flight fast and erratic. Adults feed on nectar of many flowers.

Painted Lady and West Coast Lady have four or five blue spots near rear edge of hind wing.

36

Wings orange-red with black white-spotted tips and margins, and four or five blue spots near rear edge of hind wing. Underside of wings mottled in brownish pink and white, with blue spots on margin of hind wing and red and white bars on fore wing.

Caterpillar has black head and greenish yellow body with black spots and branched spines. Feeds mostly on thistles, making nest near top of plant; also on knapweeds, burdock, and mallows.

Found in open areas and grassland. Migrate north and east in fluctuating numbers each spring from the Sonora Desert. Males perch or patrol in the afternoon. Flight straight and fast, or an erratic dance. Adults sip nectar from flowers like milkweeds and clovers.

Virginia Painted Lady: two blue spots near rear edge of hind wing. West Coast Lady: largest spot on dark wing tip, orange not white; underside of wing olive, white and brown.

Wings chocolate brown with wide yellow and reddish-orange band around the outsides; margins rather ragged, dark with blue spots. Undersides dark brown with lighter brown band on fore wings.

Caterpillar black with orange and green-yellow stripes, white spots, rows of spines and many fine hairs. Lives on nettles, at first in colonies in silken webs, later singly in folded leaves.

Found in wet meadows and river valleys, especially at higher elevations, but also seen in gardens and woodland trails. Males perch on hilltops or other high spots in the afternoon. Flight rapid and lively. Adults visit flowers like goldenrods and thistles for nectar, but also feed on fermenting fruit and sap.

California Tortoiseshell: western species with orange color on wings diffuse, not in band, margins ragged without blue spots.
Bordered Patch: wings beneath striped in brown and pale yellow.

Wings bright gold-brown with dark brown margins. Undersides of wings gray-brown with white-edged black spots near margins. Tailless.

Caterpillar green with white, yellow and green stripes and tiny yellow hairs. Caterpillar hatches in spring from egg laid the previous year on antelope bush.

Found in canyons, foothills and mountains, sage brush and pinyon pine and juniper areas. Males perch during day on shrubs on hilltops waiting for females. Adults found close to wild buckwheats and take nectar from the flowers.

Similar to many coppers but the dark front of the fore wing and the dark undersides of the wings are distinctive. Many of the other western hairstreaks lack tails.

39

Wings of male orange-brown with purple sheen and orange zigzag on hind wing; fore wings of female orange-brown with brown margins, hind wings brown with orange zigzags. Both sexes have black spots. Undersides of wings yellowish with black spots.

Caterpillar green with oblique yellow lines on the sides and many short white hairs. Feeds on docks and knotweeds.

Found in disturbed areas like roadsides, open fields and yards as well as in natural habitats from marshes to mountains, often near water. The commonest Calif. copper from sea to mountains, less common further east. Males perch in hollows waiting for females. Adults visit flowers for nectar.

Dorcas Copper: flies with Purplish Copper in the Rockies, but more common in northeast USA and eastern Canada; has less orange on the wings but the two are often indistinguishable.

Wings of male brown-violet; fore wings of female orange-brown with dark margins, hind wings brown. Both have orange margin on hind wings. Underside of hind wings white with black spots and orange margin, of fore wings orange with white margin.

Caterpillar slug-like, bright yellow-green with a dark stripe on its back. Feeds on water dock and other docks.

Found in low wet areas including wet meadows, roadside ditches and pond edges, in colonies near to its caterpillar host plants. Most common in the east, more local in the west. Males perch near caterpillar host plants, sometimes with wings open, flying up if disturbed. Adults seldom visit flowers.

American Copper: wing color brighter orange. **Purplish Copper**: underside of hind wing pale orange with orange zigzag band.

41

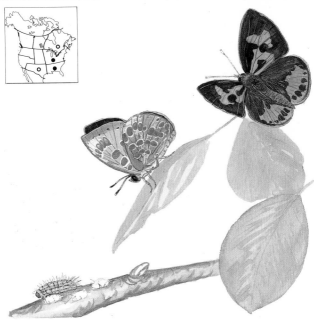

Wings orange brown with dark brown borders and blotches. Underside of fore wings brownish with yellow and brown spots, of hind wings with pattern of orange spots and circles of white scales.

Caterpillar greenish brown with long white hairs. Hides under woolly aphids and silk web on alders, also on hawthorn and beech. Feeds on the aphids and is camouflaged by them.

Found in damp deciduous woods, especially alder woods, where trees have woolly aphids. Males perch on sunlit leaves and fly at other males or patrol along paths. Flight rapid and irregular, skipping around alders, especially in hot sunshine. Males may drink at wet sand. Adults feed on aphid honeydew.

No other butterfly looks or behaves quite like a Harvester.

Distinctive butterfly with long "snout" formed of labial palps (mouthparts). Fore wings hooked but appear to be cut off at the tips, brown with orange patches and white spots. Hind wings similar but without spots.

Caterpillar dark green with yellow stripes and two yellow-circled black warts on the hump behind the head. Feeds on hackberry trees.

Found in woodland clearings and edges, never far from hackberry trees. Adults overwinter in south and huge northward migrations may occur so that butterflies obscure the sun. Flight rapid. They resemble dead leaves when perched. Males visit mud puddles. Feed on fermenting fruit and flowers.

Southern Snout Butterfly: found in canyons and washes of Arizona and Texas, orange patches on wings much paler and less well defined.

Wings patterned in bright orange, gray and brown; with brown white-spotted margins, a checkered fringe and many other white spots, including four large ones on inner fore wings.

Caterpillar purplish with short hairs growing in clusters. Feeds on many different wild buckwheats.

Found in arid places, from coastal dunes to dry rocky mountain slopes, chaparral and deserts. Perch vertically, either upright or upside down, in sunshine with wings partly open; or fly swiftly from one place to another. Adults visit flowers for nectar, especially flowers of the daisy family.

Gray Metalmark: smaller and grayer, usually seen flying around mesquite bushes.

Wings rounded, dark brown with orange bands near margin containing eyespots. Two large white-pupilled eyespots on fore wings are largest. Undersides similar but with white frosting.

Caterpillar green with a dark stripe on the back, whitish side stripes and a forked "tail." Feeds on grasses in wet meadows.

Found in arctic tundra, mountain meadows, prairie grassland and bogs. Flies in summer for only about three weeks in any one area. Males sip mud or patrol in moist meadows searching for females. Adults feed on flower nectar.

The alpines are a group of ten species with dark brown wings and eyespots. Common Alpine occurs in foothills and prairies, the others are confined to high mountains and arctic tundra.

45

Wings orange-tawny with obvious brown indented border, female darker with orange color reduced to bands in center of wings. Male has narrow black sex-brand, connected to border by broad black dash. Basks with fore wings raised, hind wings flat.

Caterpillar pale green or yellow with black head and several pale stripes on the sides. Feeds on grasses.

Found in disturbed and natural habitats, in wooded canyons and roadsides from coast to mountains in the west. More common in rural than city habitats. Males perch on ridges or in gulleys waiting for females or visit mud. Adults feed on flower nectar.

Rural Skipper is a related western skipper. It has a translucent spot on the fore wings and although found in similar places to the Woodland Skipper, it flies earlier in summer.

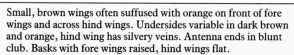

Small, brown wings often suffused with orange on front of fore wings and across hind wings. Undersides variable in dark brown and orange, hind wing has silvery veins. Antenna ends in blunt club. Basks with fore wings raised, hind wings flat.

Caterpillar green with three to seven white stripes on each side and another on the back. Feeds on grasses.

Found in short-grass prairies, mountain meadows and roadsides in northern and western prairies and Rocky Mountains. Flight weak and close to the ground amongst the grasses. Males patrol during the day in search of females.

Most other skippers have hooked antennae. Many other male skippers have black sex-brands on the fore wings.

Wings orange-brown with brown border and spots. Male has black sex-brand on fore wing with pale line in middle. Underside of hind wing has two broken crescents of pale spots or crescent and inner spot. Basks with fore wings raised, hind wings flat.

Caterpillar green and lives in silken shelter of grass leaves, low down amongst grasses. Feeds on blue grasses, fescues and brome grasses.

Found in northern grasslands, meadows, tundra, sagebrush areas and foothills. Males perch on twigs or bare ground or dart from flower to flower. Adults visit blazing stars and goldenrods for nectar.

One of many related skippers all with crescentic white markings on the hind wing underside. They include the prairie **Uncas Skipper** and the western foothills Juba Skipper.

Small, wings orange with a brassy sheen and narrow black borders. Males have narrow black sex-brand on fore wings, placed in horizontal position. Underside orange, darker on hind wings. Basks with fore wings raised, hind wings flat.

Caterpillar with a darker stripe along the back. Feeds on grasses, particularly timothy.

Found mostly in man-made habitats including grassy fields and meadows, roadsides and farms. Introduced from Europe and probably spread in hay. Now occurs in most of northeast USA and in B.C. Males patrol with steady flight, low over the ground and wandering through vegetation.

Horizontal sex-brand is distinctive. **Delaware Skipper** is bigger with wider dark brown borders.

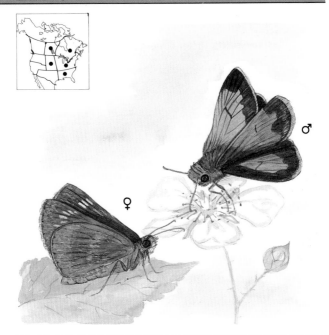

♂

♀

Wings of male yellow-orange with broad brown-black borders and long black spot near fore wing tip. Female more brown and less yellow, some almost all brown. Underside of wings has broad violet edge. Basks with fore wings raised, hind wings flat.

Caterpillar dark green to brown with transverse lines of small black tubercles with black spines. Feeds on grasses.

Found in clearings and edges of moist deciduous woods and valleys, meadows and hedges. Males perch on or close to ground in woodland clearings, while females frequent open meadows, sometimes a considerable distance from woods. Adults visit flowers like blackberries, henbit and milkweeds for nectar.

Southern Golden Skipper is very similar, but all females are dark brown; found in southeastern woods.

50

Wings of male bright orange with indented brown-black border, spots and large black sex-brand on fore wing. Female brown with large orange spots. Underside yellow-brown with dark spots. Antenna short. Basks with fore wings raised, hind wings flat.

Caterpillar brown with three dark longitudinal stripes. Lives in horizontal shelter amongst grass roots. Lawn pest in south, for so close to the ground it is unaffected by lawn mowers.

Found in open grassy areas including meadows, roadsides, lawns, more successful in man-made habitats than in natural ones. Resident in the south and migrate north each summer in the east. Males perch on low vegetation and fly out at passing insects. Adults visit many flowers for nectar.

Other small orange skippers have longer antennae and have no brown spots on undersides of wings. **Sachem**: male lacks black borders, female has translucent spots on fore wings.

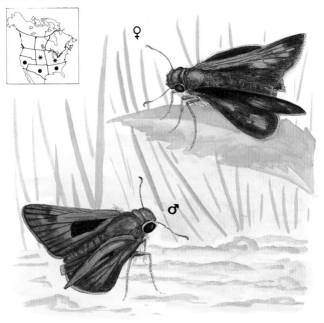

Wings orange-brown; male has very large black sex-brands on fore wings. Female often darker brown, with translucent spot in center of fore wing. Underside of wings yellow and brown. Basks with fore wings raised, hind wings flat.

Caterpillar olive-green with darker green line on back. It has many tiny black tubercles with short black hairs. Lives in silk tent at grass roots and feeds on grasses.

Found in lawns and back yards, disturbed areas, roadsides, fields and pastures. Resident in southern USA and migrate north in summer. Males perch for most of the day close to or on the ground in grassland. Adults visit yellow flowers of the daisy family, also milkweeds and thistles for nectar.

Fiery Skipper: male has dark border, female lacks translucent spots.

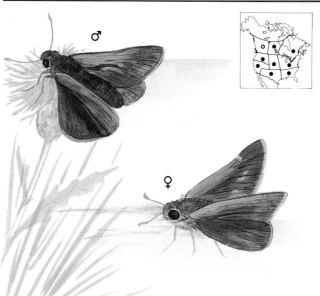

Wings olive-brown with orange-tawny edges to fore wings. Male has black sex-brand on fore wing in reverse S-shape. Female has yellow spots on fore wing. Underside tawny yellow to mustard. Basks with fore wings raised, hind wings flat.

Caterpillar yellow-brown to dark brown covered with spiny black hairs. Head is black with conspicuous light stripes. Feeds on grasses.

Found in moist grassland in the east, in forest clearings in the west, much commoner in east and rare in northwest. Males perch close to the ground in grassland and valleys for most of the day. Adults visit many flowers for nectar including dogbane, clover, alfalfa and thistles.

One of several similar related skippers difficult to distinguish from one another. **Yellowpatch Skipper**, Crossline Skipper and Long Dash are amongst them.

Wings gray-brown with orange margins on rear of hind wings, more obvious on female. She also has black spots on fore wing. Undersides of wings pale gray with black spots and orange margins on hind wings, wider in east than west populations.

Caterpillar green with dark stripe on the back. Feeds on broad dock in the prairies and on desert rhubarb in the west.

Found in two areas, separated by Rockies; in foothills, dry flats and grasslands in Oregon and Calif. and on prairies. Males perch on flowers with wings partly spread and fly at passing insects; they may chase each other for some way with jerky flight until one returns. Adults visit flowers often.

Edith's Copper: smaller species from mountain meadows, dry stream beds and open sagebrush of Rockies; female brown, male brown with yellow marks and margins.

♀

♂

Tailless. Wings gray-brown and female often has orange spots along edge of hind wing. Underside of hind wing has conspicuous row of large red-orange spots along margin as well as black white-edged spots.

Caterpillar green and pink. Hatches in spring from eggs laid previous year. Feeds on flowers and fruits of wild plums and cherries and often tended by ants.

Found in open woodland, clearings, roadsides, often in canyons in the west, always near to wild plum or cherry trees and most common in east. Males perch on hilltops or small trees in the middle of the day and attack other males and insects. Adults feed on nectar of butterflyweed, and bee plant in the west.

Arcadian Hairstreak has tails. No other tailless hairstreak has row of orange spots.

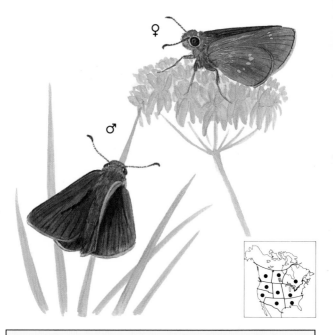

♀

♂

Wings brown-black, male plain but for black sex-brand on fore wing. Few white spots on female fore wings. Underside dark yellow-brown, with crescent of pale spots in female. Orange scales on head. Basks with fore wings raised, hind wings flat.

Caterpillar translucent green with many silvery white markings. Feeds on sedges or grasses.

Found in wet areas in deciduous woods like powerline cuts, marshes, roadsides and logging trails. Males perch in open areas about three feet above ground, especially in late afternoon or visit areas of wet mud to drink. Adults nectar at pink or purple flowers including mints, dogbane and milkweeds.

Northern Broken Dash has larger yellow spots on fore wings and both it and **Little Glassy Wing** have purple-brown undersides to hind wings.

56

Wings dark brown with row of glassy white spots on both sides of fore wings, one square spot larger than others. Male sex-brand adjoins spots. Underside of hind wings purple-brown, darker in female. Basks with fore wings raised, hind wings flat.

Caterpillar yellow-green to yellow-brown with many tiny brown spots and pale hairs. It has several dark stripes on back and sides. Feeds on desert bunchgrass.

Found in moist woods, in clearings and edges, also in fields and meadows, in bogs and near streams. Males most often found in sunlit woodland clearings perched on low vegetation. Adults visit pink or purple flowers for nectar, including milkweeds, dogbane and peppermint.

Dun Skipper and **Northern Broken Dash** lack glassy spots on fore wings.

Wings brown with a few small yellow spots. Male has black sex-brand on fore wing, broken into two by patch of shiny scales. Underside of hind wings purple-brown with faint crescent of paler spots. Basks with fore wings raised, hind wings flat.

Caterpillar pale green, mottled with dark green and with a dark green line on the back. Feeds on panic grasses.

Found in brush or open woods, open fields or areas near woods. Males perch on branches three to six feet above the ground. Seldom flies far when disturbed, less active than many skippers. Adults visit pink or purple flowers for nectar, including dogbane, red clover and New Jersey tea.

Broken Dash: from southern USA, smaller with more yellow on wings. **Little Glassy Wing**: row of glassy spots on fore wings. **Dun Skipper**: undersides of wings dark yellow-brown.

58

Wings brown-black with several tiny translucent spots on both sides near tips of pointed fore wings. Underside of wings dusted with gray-violet scales on outer edges. Male has no sex-brand. Basks with fore wings raised, hind wings flat.

Caterpillar pale mauve above, gray below and covered with long yellowish hairs. Lives in tent of leaves bound with silk at base of foodplant, which is beard grass.

Found in sandy pine barrens and burned ground colonized by beard grass. The grass grows in burnt areas until succeeded by other species, so the butterfly is only found in an area following a fire for a few years. In pine barrens the grass grows permanently. Male perches on bare ground in sunshine.

There are several related southwestern skippers living in deserts and canyons, mostly with gray-brown wings. Most other male skippers have sex-brand.

Wings rounded, lusterless dark brown to black with cluster of tiny white spots near fore wing tip. Underside of wings dark brown, with violet-gray scales on fore wing tip and outer half of hind wing. Basks with fore wings raised, hind wings flat.

Caterpillar pale green with many green spots and tiny hairs. It is covered with a waxy white powder. Feeds on grasses, including Kentucky blue grass, bent grass and wild oats.

Found in clearings in moist woods, ravines, roadsides and canyons, most often near streams. More common in the north than in the south. Males perch on rocks or on the ground. Adults fly rapidly, close to the ground, and visit flowers infrequently.

One of a group of related skippers, mostly local in their ranges, but found throughout N. America. Mottled Roadside Skipper: mottled undersides, lives in lawns in southern USA.

Wings gray-brown with three to five small translucent white spots in center of fore wing, on both sides. Underside of wings brown, dusted with gray scales on hind wings. Basks with fore wings raised, hind wings flat.

Caterpillar vivid green with darker stripe on the back and yellowish stripes on the sides. Feeds on grasses.

Found in open areas, including hills and fields, roadsides, deserts and vacant lots. Males perch on low-growing plants in flat grassy places waiting for females. Adults visit several flowers for nectar including croton, alfalfa and flowers of the daisy family.

Other small dark skippers are generally less gray and more brown in color.

Fore wings long, dark brown with a row of glassy yellow spots across center on both sides. Hind wings notched, brown with a large central irregular silver spot on underside. Basks with wings spread flat, in triangular position.

Caterpillar yellow-green with yellow spots and cross-lines. Lives in leaf shelter on foodplants, including small locust trees, wisteria and other legumes.

Found in open brush and woodland near locust trees, in parks and back yards often near wisteria. Males perch on branches up to ten feet above ground and may have spectacular aerial encounters with other males. Flight rapid and erratic. Adults visit pink or blue flowers, like vetches and milkweeds.

Golden-banded and **Hoary-edged Skippers** lack silver spot on underside of hind wing.

Wings dark brown to black with two curved rows of small white spots on each fore wing. Undersides of wings are dark brown.

Caterpillar pale green, flecked with lighter spots. Feeds on weeds like lamb's quarters, goosefoots and pigweeds. Makes a shelter from a folded leaf, bound with silk into a cylinder.

Found in disturbed ground, farmyards, vacant lots, roadsides as well as fields, river banks and cultivated land. Males patrol most of the day. Flight rapid and zigzagging, only a few inches from the ground. They may visit wet spots on dirt roads, also visit clovers, dogbane and milkweeds for nectar.

Other sootywings live in desert areas of west and southwest. Great Basin Sootywing has white spots on undersides of wings. Saltbush Sootywing has dark arrow-shaped marks on fore wings.

Wings rounded, brown with many glassy white, somewhat triangular spots in very broken diagonal bands across both sides of fore wings. Undersides of wings frosted with gray scales.

Caterpillar dark purplish green with pink lines on sides and many minute orange warts, each with one hair. Lives in silken nest amongst leaves of legumes like clovers and bush clovers.

Found in open woods and brush, roadsides, fields and meadows, where clovers grow. Males perch on or close to ground along forest trails or in clearings, or visit wet ground beside streams. Flight strong and erratic and close to ground. Adults visit pink or blue flowers like clover, milkweeds and dogbane.

Southern Cloudywing has hourglass-shaped spot on fore wing. Eastern Cloudywing difficult to distinguish, spots on fore wing linear rather than triangular.

Wings dark gray with conspicuous black bands and tiny white spots on the upper surface of the fore wings. Margins of hind wings scalloped.

Caterpillar deep green with a rosy hue and many fine white hairs. Lives in silken leaf shelters and feeds at night on lamb's quarters, goosefoots and amaranths.

Found in vacant lots, weedy disturbed ground, suburban back yards, also in moist open woodland. Males perch on low vegetation in broken sunlight. Adults visit clovers, sweet clovers, dogbane and other flowers for nectar.

Southern Scalloped Sootywing: almost black, with less distinct banding on wings.

Wings of male black-brown; fore wings with dark markings and eight whitish, glassy spots, hind wings with long gray hairs. Female lighter brown with similar markings.

Caterpillar pale green with white hairy tubercles. Feeds on leaves of black oak, red oak and white oak.

Found in oak woods, chaparral with scrub oak and adjacent fields, roadsides and meadows. Males perch on twigs up to 12 feet above ground along forest trails and woodland edges or patrol. Also visit wet spots along streams or trails. Adults nectar at many plants like blueberries, wild plum and redbud.

Rocky Mountain Duskywing: very similar, found in oak woods in Rockies. Horace's Duskywing: also similar, found in Rockies, Canada and eastern USA, has six white spots on fore wing.

Wings brown with black "chain-link" and other markings across fore wings. Hind wings plain but for pale spots near margin.

Caterpillar pale green with white hairy tubercles. Feeds on oak leaves, usually bear oak and scrub oak.

Found in areas where scrubby oaks are common, in foothills and chaparral, also in sandy and serpentine barrens. Males perch during day on hilltops waiting for females or patrol around caterpillar foodplants. Adults visit heathland plants like blueberries and wild azaleas for nectar.

Dreamy Duskywing: very similar, found in northern USA and Canada in clearings and trails of northern forests.

Wings of male olive-brown with dark veins, five or six dark spots between the veins on hind wings; fore wings have one black eyespot and black white-spotted tips. Female similar but larger and more tawny. Underside patterned in purple and white.

Caterpillar greenish yellow, tapered at both ends, with two tails at rear end and horns on head. Feeds on hackberry leaves. Overwinters on leaves on ground and climbs tree in spring.

Found near hackberry trees along woodland trails, on riversides and woodland edges; also in cities and parks if hackberry trees are present. Flight fast and erratic. Adults rest on trees, often high up. They feed on rotting fruit, sap and manure.

Tawny Emperor: orange-brown wings with black markings, spots on dark wing tip yellow. Related southern hackberry butterflies are distinguished by differences in markings and eyespots.

Wings dusky orange-brown with dark checkered, smudged markings and interrupted lines of metallic marks around outer sides of wings.

Caterpillar green with black spots and long white hairs on its back. Feeds on the leaves of ragwort.

Found in open woods and on hillsides, usually near shale or limestone rocks and streams. Three areas, in central Kentucky, in Appalachians, and Indiana and Ohio. Perch in sun on broad leaves with wings at 150°. On dull days or if disturbed they perch upside down beneath leaves. Adults visit flowers often.

One of several similar metalmarks. They are very local and specific in their habitat needs. Found in southeastern deserts, in the southeast and Calif. Some are more orange in color.

♂

♀

Wings of male brown, female red-brown. Undersides of wings gray-brown, criss-crossed with dark veins and banded with irregular black and white lines. Wing margins appear scalloped.

Caterpillar green with white stripes, camouflaged amongst young pine needles on which it feeds. Foodplants are young hard pine trees.

Found in open pine woods, in clearings and on roadsides in forests. Males perch in trees, up to ten feet above ground or gather at mud puddles or stream sides. Flight leisurely. Adults nectar at flowers of wild plum, blackberry, blueberry. Females may be disturbed into flight by a blow to a pine tree.

Western Pine Elfin: similar species found in pine forests of the west, on both sides of the Rockies.

A plain butterfly with brown wings. Reddish-brown on undersides with no white markings and no tails.

Caterpillar bright green with yellow-green stripe on back and oblique stripes on sides. Feeds on flowers and fruits of heath family, including blueberries, bearberry and azaleas.

Found in open pine barrens, coniferous woodland, chaparral, acid bogs and also in parks. Males perch on shrubs or in clearings, or sun themselves on stones. Flight feeble and close to the ground. Adults visit variety of flowers for nectar, including bearberries, wild plum and spicebush.

There are several other similar elfins, like Henry's, Hoary and Early Elfins, but all have some white frosting on the undersides of the hind wings.

Wings plain dark brown with tiny spots or no spots at all. Undersides of wings brown with many white scales and yellow-rimmed eyespots, six on hind wing, of which second and fifth are darkest and most pronounced.

Caterpillar light green with dark green longitudinal stripes. It has many tubercles with short yellow hairs. Feeds on grasses including carpet grass and centipede grass.

Found in deciduous woods, usually at lower altitudes and near water, as in the Mississippi river valley. Males patrol with relatively slow weak flight. They perch on forest grasses or on the ground or visit mud. Adults feed on rotting fruit and sap.

Other similar satyrs have eyespots on upper surface of fore wings except Hermes Satyr, a southwestern species which cannot easily be distinguished.

Wings orange-brown without eyespots. Underside of fore wings similar, sometimes with one eyespot near the wing tip; of hind wings gray-green, lighter towards the margins and with a pale streak across the center.

Caterpillar long and slender with many short hairs and a very short forked "tail." It is dark green with longitudinal whitish stripes on the sides. Feeds on grasses.

Found in prairie grassland, meadows, open grassy areas in woods and on embankments. Males patrol with dancing jerky flight above the grass. Adults visit flowers for nectar, including yellow flowers of the daisy family.

One of several similar "Tullia" ringlets found throughout N. America, except the far north and southeast. Ocher Ringlet from the Rockies has eyespots on underside of hind wings.

Wings yellow-brown with two or three eyespots on the fore wing and one on the hind wing. Inner part of male fore wing darker. Underside of fore wing yellowish, of hind wing patterned in brown with dark central streak.

Caterpillar greenish-brown with longitudinal stripes of yellow, green and brown. Feeds on grasses.

Found in arctic tundra, mountain slopes and meadows, forest clearings, northern prairies and grassland. Markings on undersides of wings provide perfect camouflage when butterflies land. They fly low, often a short rapid flight, and land suddenly. Males perch on hillsides waiting for females.

Arctics are a group of species all with yellow-brown or brown wings and cryptic colors on the wing undersides. All but the Chryxus are confined to high mountains or arctic tundra.

Wings rounded, dull brown. There are two yellow-rimmed black eyespots on each wing. Undersides similar but with smaller eyespots as well, and wavy darker lines.

Caterpillar light brown with a black stripe on the back, covered with tiny white tubercles each with a single brown hair and with a white forked "tail." Feeds on grasses.

Found in woods and on woodland edges, meadows and even in city parks. Males patrol woodland trails and edges in sunshine or bask with open wings on woodland floor or on leaves. Flight slow and dancing, often near the ground but may be near tree tops. Adults feed on sap and aphid honeydew, also on nectar.

Carolina Satyr: lacks spots on upper surface of wings.

75

Wings light to dark brown; fore wings have two large black yellow-rimmed eyespots often in band of yellow. Underside of hind wings has darker inner and lighter outer areas with up to six eyespots.

Caterpillar green with many short yellow hairs, four pale longitudinal stripes and a reddish forked "tail." Feeds on grasses.

Found in open woodland with grassy clearings, in prairies, meadows, grassy riversides, marshes and old fields. Only Wood Nymph found east of the Mississippi. Males have irregular jumping flight but females are less active, often resting in shade. Exposes eyespots if startled. Adults feed little.

Several similar related western Wood Nymphs including Red-eyed Wood Nymph, a Rocky Mountain species with reddish fore wings. Great Basin Wood Nymph: fore wings lack yellow band.

Wings scalloped, light brown with row of prominent dark brown spots around edges, four spots on fore wing, five on hind wing. Undersides brown with yellow-rimmed eyespots, seven on hind wing. Antennae have black clubs.

Caterpillar green with dark green and yellow stripes, red-tipped horns on the head and a forked "tail" with pink tips. Feeds on various forest grasses.

Found in local colonies in deciduous forest clearings and on woodland edges, especially near streams in mountains: further north in open wet woods and marshes. Adults perch on tree trunks or feed at sap flows on willow, birch or poplar. Males may dart out at passing insects. Flight swift and erratic.

Pearly Eye: orange clubs on antennae. Creole Pearly Eye: five spots on fore wing. Both these species are found near cane, the caterpillar host plant, in shady southeastern woods.

77

Wings rounded rather than scalloped, warm brown with dark eyespots near outer margin. Underside light brown with yellow-rimmed dark eyespots and zigzag lines.

Caterpillar light green with dark green longitudinal stripes. It has two red-tipped "horns" on the head and a forked red-tipped "tail." Feeds on sedges.

Found in local colonies in wet prairie grassland and damp meadows, also on the margins of freshwater cat-tail marshes. Threatened by drainage schemes in many places. Flight dancing and close to the gound. Males perch on low vegetation and bask in the sunshine. Adults feed on sap or bird droppings.

Appalachian Eyed Brown: darker in color, with wavy, not zigzag lines, on underside. **Pearly Eyes** have scalloped wing edges and are forest species.

Wings scalloped but with pointed fore wing tip; brown with two large eyespots and two small eyespots on each side. There are two forms; wings of smaller summer form brown beneath, wings of larger winter form dull red beneath.

Caterpillar black with broken yellow and orange lines along sides, orange head and spiky black spines. Found singly on foodplants including plantain, snapdragon, foxglove and toadflax.

Found in open places, roads and railroads, parks and meadows, fields and dunes. Resident in south and migrate north in summer. Flight fast and straight, flapping and then sailing. Aggressive, perching on tall plants, chasing butterflies and large insects. Adults visit flowers like asters, chicory, knapweeds for nectar.

Caribbean Buckeye: three of the four eyespots nearly equal in size. Dark Buckeye: nearly black with small blue-centered eyespots, found in canyons of southwest USA in fall.

BRAMBLE GREEN HAIRSTREAK
(Calif.) Feb–Apr; (N) May–Jun

1in

Wings gray-brown. Underside of hind wings green, of fore wings brown and green. There are faint white spots on underside of hind wings.

Caterpillar green with or without white stripes on the sides and tiny brown hairs. Feeds on deer weed and Californian buckwheat.

Found in dry western wasteland, rocky hills and chaparral, also in canyons and dunes, and east into the mountains. Furthest north it occurs in the glades of coniferous forests. Males perch on hilltops, or bare ground of paths or on branches. Adults visit wild buckwheat flowers for nectar.

One of several similar western green hairstreaks difficult to distinguish from each other. Most others have more conspicuous white spots on the undersides of the hind wings.

Fore wings brown with rectangular whitish spots; hind wings have long tails. Head, thorax, bases of fore wings and hind wings have iridescent green sheen. Underside of wings brown with white spots on fore wing and lighter bands on hind wing.

Caterpillar yellow-green with black, yellow and green stripes. Lives in rolled leaves on cultivated beans and other legumes. Occasional pest in southern USA, called the Bean Leaf Roller.

Found in open woods, brush, gardens and open disturbed ground. Males perch along woodland edges, up to six feet above ground. Flight slow and hovering as if the tails were heavy, or fast and close to the ground. Adults roost upside down under leaves. They feed on nectar of lantana and bougainvillea.

Other longtail skippers, like the Lilac-banded Longtail, occur in southern states, but they are brown and none have the iridescent head and wings of this species.

Black wings, with red stripe across fore wings and along base of hind wings, white spots on wing tip and broken white line around wings. Undersides of wings mottled in brown, black and blue with a red bar across the fore wing.

Caterpillars vary from black to brown or light green, often with yellow spots and warts or spines. Live in curled leaves, mostly on plants of the nettle family but also on hops.

Found in woodland, on woodland edges, roadsides and back yards, farms and meadows. Many southern butterflies migrate north in spring to supplement the northern populations. Males territorial and perch in the afternoon on hilltops or roofs. Flight fast and erratic. Nectar on flowers or feed on fermenting fruit.

No other butterfly is quite like this one. **Painted Lady** has orange-red wings with black wing tips. **Milbert's Tortoiseshell** has brown wings with wide yellow-orange bands around margins.

Wings black with a crescent-shaped band of white rectangles across center and diffuse orange tips to the fore wings. Underside of wings orange-red and black with a band of white spots across center.

Caterpillar mottled olive-green to brown with a white patch on the back and a light band on the side. Feeds on willows, poplars and cottonwoods.

Found in mountain canyons, river valleys, marshes, near canals and lakes, wherever willows or cottonwoods grow. Adults bask in sunshine, on protruding branches, opening and closing their wings, and males often fly out at passing insects. Flight alternately flapping and gliding.

Calif. Sister: red patch on fore wing sharply defined and rounded. Weidemeyer's Admiral (found near willows in midwest) and **White Admiral** are larger and lack red wing tips.

◆ WHITE ADMIRAL
Jun–Jul & Aug–Oct

3in

Two forms: typical form has black wings with broad white stripe and blue-white crescents around edges. Red-spotted Purple form has black wings, diffuse blue stripe and crescents near edges, and red spots on underside; it mimics Pipevine Swallowtail.

Caterpillar of both forms grotesque, with hump behind head. Typical form mottled greenish-yellow, Red-spotted Purple form cream-colored with dark saddle. Feeds on willows and birches.

Typical form found on forest paths and edges in southern Canada and northeastern USA. Red-spotted Purple form found in open mixed deciduous woods and meadows mainly in more southern areas of USA. Flight slow, alternately flapping and sailing. Males attracted to wet soil. Feed on carrion, rotting fruit and sap.

Pipevine Swallowtail: Red-spotted Purple mimics this butterfly which is black with blue margins. **Lorquin's Admiral**: west coast species, like typical form but with orange-tipped wings.

Wings triangular with long white-bordered tails. Blue-white with
vertical black stripes and a black border with white crescents or
spots, red spot on corner of hind wing. Underside black and white
with central stripe on hind wing.

Caterpillar green with transverse yellow and black stripes and a
swollen black front end. Foodplant is pawpaw.

Found in open brush, neglected fields and wet woods near rivers
or lakes, never far from pawpaws. Flight fast and direct, quick to
dart away. Frequent visitor to flowers like blackberry and
blueberry, milkweeds and verbena. Males gather at wet sand and
along stream banks, especially in spring.

Pale Tiger Swallowtail: western mountain species with white and
black vertical stripes. **Two-tailed Western Swallowtail:** western
canyon and mountain species with two tails.

A distinctively shaped butterfly, with long narrow fore wings, black with horizontal light yellow bands. It is distasteful to birds, containing poisons from passion flower vines, retained from the caterpillar.

Caterpillar white with six rows of black spines. Feeds on young leaves of poisonous passion flower vines. Caterpillars retain poisons in their bodies and pass them to the adults.

Found in thickets and hammocks, forest edges and glades in southern USA, spreading north in summer into the plains and Calif. Flight slow and feeble. They live for up to six months, setting up a "trap-line," plants from which they take pollen. Gather in groups at dusk in woodland and roost in the trees.

No other similar butterfly.

♀

Wings black, yellowish near base, with yellow bands on outer fore wings and diffuse yellow margin on hind wings. Undersides dark with white frosting and spots. Body large and rounded.

Caterpillar white with black head. Feeds on yuccas, at first in the leaf apex, making a silk tent at the point of entry, later boring into the plant to reach the roots.

The most widely distributed giant skipper. Found in old fields, pine woods, granite outcrops, bottomlands and dunes where yuccas are growing. Flight extremely fast. Males, at least in the west, are territorial. They perch high up in the mornings waiting for females or may visit wet sand to drink.

There are several giant skippers in southern USA. Most, like Calif. Giant Skipper, have brown wings. **Orange Giant Skipper** from southwestern mountains is orange.

Wings black with two rows of cream-colored spots and a row of chevrons on rim; hind wings have blue center, larger in female. Both sexes have a red black-centered spot at the corner of each hind wing. Abdomen has creamy spots on side.

Caterpillar transversely striped in greenish white and black with yellow spots. Feeds on wild carrot, dill, parsnip and other members of carrot family. May be a pest in gardens.

Found in open spaces, farmland and meadows; may be attracted to garden vegetables. Flight strong and rapid or slow and drifting amongst nectar plants like thistles and milkweeds. May also drink at puddles. In afternoon males perch on low shrubs or hilltops and patrol in search of females.

Western Black Swallowtail: similar butterfly in arid areas of west. **Anise Swallowtail**: fore wings more yellow than black. **Spicebush Swallowtail**: one row of creamy spots.

Wings black-brown with two rows of yellow spots, one row horizontal and the other inside the wing margins, converging near the tips of the fore wings. Orange spot at corner of hind wing. Single yellow spot on each tail.

Caterpillar known as "Orange Dog", olive-brown and white, like large bird dropping with orange "horns" which release pungent odor. Feeds at night on prickly ash and citrus trees.

Found in open brush, pine woods, citrus groves and towns, most common in the south. Flight strong and leisurely, often gliding for long distances. Males patrol open areas in woods or along river edges or may be seen drinking at wet mud or sand. Adults feed on sap and manure.

No other swallowtail has the horizontal yellow row of spots. **Black Swallowtails** and **Shorttail Black Swallowtail** have metallic blue areas on hind wings.

89

ANISE SWALLOWTAIL
Spring, summer & fall

2½–3in

Fore wings have broad yellow band and appear more yellow than black. Hind wings similar with a row of blue blotches and a red black-centered spot at corner of each. Underside similar in pattern and colors. Abdomen black with yellow side stripes.

Caterpillar green with transverse yellow-spotted black bands. Feeds on plants of carrot family, from carrots and parsley to fennel and cow parsnip. Can be pest on citrus trees in Calif.

Found in open spaces from western seashores and mountains, to disturbed ground and vacant city lots where fennel is growing, but scarce in deserts of southwest. Males perch on hilltops or tops of shrubs to watch for females and pursue them for some distance. Also visit mud puddles.

Western Tiger Swallowtail: wings yellow with black patches and margins. Desert Swallowtail: southwestern deserts in canyons and washes. Oregon Swallowtail: arid areas of northwest USA.

TIGER SWALLOWTAIL

3–5½in   (S) spring–fall; (N) summer

Wings yellow with three broad black vertical stripes and a black border. Hind wings have red spot at base. Some females (most common in Carolinas) are black with a row of metallic blue patches on hind wings to mimic Pipe Vine Swallowtail.

Caterpillar dark green with two large eyespots on swollen front end. Feeds at night on variety of broadleaf trees, like cherries, willows and cottonwoods. Spends day in curled leaf.

Found in city trees and deciduous woods, most often along streams and rivers and in wooded swamps, often about the tops of trees. Males patrol in afternoon along streams or woodland roads and collect at mud puddles or streams. Flight more leisurely than many swallowtails. Frequent visitor to flowers.

Pipe Vine Swallowtail: no red spot at base of hind wing. Black female also resembles **Spicebush Swallowtail** but this has a row of blue-white crescentic spots around wing margins.

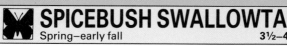

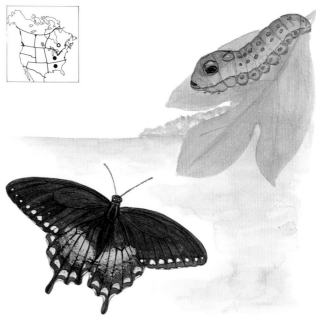

Wings brown-black with row of white spots round margin of fore wings and blue-white crescents round margin of hind wings. Hind wings have orange spot at corner and are suffused with metallic blue in male. Both sexes mimic Pipe Vine Swallowtail.

Caterpillar green with two eyespots on swollen front end and two orange spots behind them. Shelters in curled leaf by day, feeding at night on sassafras and spice bushes.

Found in wet deciduous woodland and woodland edges, pine barrens, meadows and back yards. Flight fast, direct and nervous but a frequent visitor to flowers, especially honeysuckle and jewelweed. Males patrol open areas in woods in search of females.

Pipe Vine Swallowtail: no orange spot at base of hind wing. **Black Swallowtails**: red spot at corner of hind wing black-centered. Dark female **Tiger Swallowtails** are bluer.

Fore wings long and black. Hind wings metallic blue with short tails and a line of white spots but no red spot at corner. Underside of each hind wing has semi-circle of seven black-bordered red spots.

Caterpillar reddish black with rows of red tubercles. Feeds on pipe vines. These contain poisons which are retained by the caterpillar and pass to adult making it distasteful to birds.

Found most commonly in Appalachian forests but also in back yards and roadsides, orchards and meadows, where pipe vines are cultivated. Flight strong, low over ground. Males gather at wet sand or mud on country roads and patrol in afternoon. Adults feed on nectar of many flowers, especially thistles.

Mimicked by several butterflies including **Eastern Black**, **Tiger** and **Spicebush Swallowtails**, Diana Fritillary and **Red-spotted Purple** but none have the spots on underside of hind wing.

COMMON BLUE
Apr–Aug

1–1½in

Wings of male silver blue or dark blue with dark margins, female brown or with bluish wing bases. Undersides pale gray to brownish with large white-ringed black spots on fore wing and smaller white-ringed black, or white spots on hind wing.

Caterpillar green with many white hairs. Feeds on lupines, always the hairiest lupine in the area, and tended by ants which make an entrance to the nest at the base of the plant.

Found in colonies in a variety of habitats from mountain meadows, roadsides and valleys, sage brush and coastal dunes, but always close to lupines. Males patrol near caterpillar host plants or may be seen at mud puddles.

Several other very similar blues. **Silvery Blue**: single crooked row of prominent white-rimmed black spots on undersides of both wings. **Greenish Blue**: wing spots not white-ringed.

Male has silver blue wings with narrow black border, female brown or gray with wider dark margins. Undersides steel gray with line of white-rimmed black spots near margins of both wings with no other marks to the outside.

Caterpillar slug-like, varying in color from pale green to purplish with dark stripe on back and oblique side stripes. Feeds on flowers and pods of legumes. Tended by ants.

Found in wide variety of habitats from clearings in woods, to meadows, streamsides and disturbed areas, in lowlands and mountains. Amongst the first butterflies to appear in spring. Males patrol near the caterpillar foodplant. Flight rapid. Adults visit flowers of the daisy family.

No other blues have the distinctive single row of white-rimmed black spots near the margin of both wings with no other marks to the outside.

GREENISH BLUE

Jun–Jul

1–1¼in

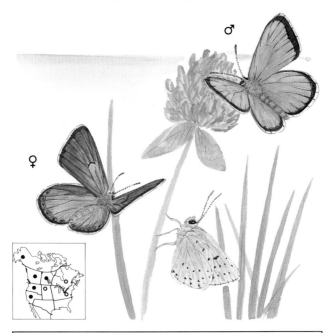

Male has silver blue wings with dark margins; female brown or blue, sometimes with orange area near base of tail. Underside of wings of male silver-gray, of female browner. Both sexes have scattered black spots on undersides of both wings.

Caterpillar green or red, hibernates when half grown. Feeds on flowers of many clovers.

Found in wet places where clovers grow, meadows, roadsides, prairies and edges of tundra, bogs in the east. Common in the west, in scattered colonies in the east. Adult males patrol close to the ground near the clovers and congregate along streams and trails in damp places.

One of several related blues difficult to distinguish from one another. **Common Blue**: white-rimmed black spots on hind wing smaller than those on fore wing.

96

Wings of male bright blue with black margins; female brown, some with bluish wing bases. Both sexes have band of orange on hind wings. Undersides gray-white with black spots, and row of orange spots on hind wing capped with metallic green scales.

Caterpillar dirty yellow with white hairs and a green stripe on the back. Feeds on variety of legumes, including locoweeds, deer weed and lupines, also on wild buckwheats.

Found in a wide variety of habitats throughout the west except in deserts and cities. They fly close to the ground. Wings flash with metallic green glints in the sun as they twitch, especially noticeable while males drink at mud puddles, along forest trails for example.

Dotted Blue and its relatives do not have metallic green scales. Lupine Blue: almost indistinguishable, found in southwestern mountains. **Melissa Blue** female: more orange on wings.

Male silver or dark blue with narrow black margins. Female slate gray with orange borders. Undersides of wings generally suffused with orange, with bold orange spots and bold black line around margin.

Caterpillar green with short brown hairs and faint oblique side stripes. Feeds on young leaves of many legumes, like lupines, alfalfa and wild licorice. Tended by ants.

Found in open areas, dry mountain meadows in the west, alfalfa fields, dry prairies, and pine barrens and dunes in the east. Common and widespread in west, declining and endangered in east. Males patrol near caterpillar host plants in daylight hours, flying near to the ground, or gather at mud puddles.

Northern Blue and **Acmon Blue** have less orange on the wings. Acmon Blues flash metallic green in the sun.

♂

♀

Male has bright blue wings with black margins; female dark brown with orange spots on rear margins of hind wings. Undersides light gray with orange spots on hind wing and many heavy black spots.

Caterpillar slug-like, creamy white with pink and brown marks, camouflaged amongst flowers of foodplants. Feeds on buds and flowers of wild buckwheats.

Found in a variety of habitats, near to wild buckwheats, usually in arid, rocky and desert areas, in western lowlands and mountains. Fly only when these caterpillar foodplants are in flower, for about a month in any one locality, laying their eggs in the flowers. Often seen perching on the plants.

Several similar blues are associated with wild buckwheats, including Square-spotted, Rita's and Pale Blues. **Acmon Blue** is commoner, undersides of hind wings flash green in the sun.

SPRING AZURE

Spring—fall

¾–1¼in

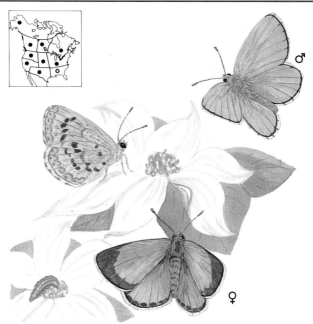

Wings blue in spring form, pale whitish blue in summer form; male has narrow black border, female black border on fore wing and black spots on rear of hind wing. Underside slate gray with dark markings in spring form, much paler in summer.

Caterpillar velvety yellow-cream to pink, with oblique green side stripes. Feeds on flowers of trees with flower clusters, like dogwood, cherry and New Jersey tea. Often tended by ants.

Found in or near open woodland and brush, where caterpillar host plants occur. Males patrol, flying about three feet above the ground, mostly in afternoon. Adults also flutter higher up, near the flowers of the trees. Males gather at wet soil on roads and along streams. Often the first butterfly of spring.

Most other blues have deeper blue wings with brown or pale gray undersides, and have spots rather than the gray markings of the Spring Azure.

Wings of male silver blue with orange and black spots; wings of female gray, bluer in spring form. Both sexes have small tails. Undersides of wings gray-white.

Caterpillar dark green with small tubercles and fine hairs, brown stripe on the back and faint oblique side stripes. Feeds on flowers and pods of clovers, beans and other legumes.

Found in open sunny areas where clovers and trefoils grow, weedy meadows, roadsides and railroads, gardens. Males patrol with rapid, skipping flight, landing frequently and twitching their wings when perched as when gathered at mud puddles. Take nectar from many flowers like clovers, cinquefoils and asters.

Western Tailed Blue: only other blue with tails, larger and undersides of wings chalk white; found in meadows, roadsides, clearings in Pacific states, western mountains and northwest.

Wings black, males dark brown beneath, females slate gray beneath. Undersides of wings have lines of dark white-edged rectangles. There is a blue spot near the tail.

Caterpillar green or brown, with lighter or darker lines and fine brown hairs. Hatches in spring from egg laid in previous year. Feeds on catkins and leaves of oak, hickory and walnut.

Found in deciduous forests, in woodland edges and clearings, roads and railroads, along power lines and in city parks. Males perch on sunlit shrubs and trees and engage others in territorial battles. Adults visit a variety of flowers but especially dogbane and milkweeds.

Striped Hairstreak: rectangles on underside of wing are wider. Edward's Hairstreak: underside line formed of ovals, not rectangles. Hickory Hairstreak: line of rectangles double.

THICKET HAIRSTREAK

1–1¼in   (Calif.) Mar–Sep; (N) Jun–Jul

Wings steel blue-gray. Underside of wings red-brown to brown with white-edged line near margins forming a "W" on hind wings.

Caterpillar green with red, white and yellow marks and many bumps and ridges. Well camouflaged on foodplants which are dwarf mistletoes, parasitic on conifers.

Found in clearings and canyons in coniferous woodland on both sides of the Rocky Mountains. Flight fast and erratic. Males perch on hilltops and shrubs waiting for females or visit mud puddles. Adults feed on nectar of wild buckwheats and flowers of the daisy family.

Several related hairstreaks have brown wings with similar undersides. Loki's and Juniper Hairstreak live close to junipers, Nelson's and Olive Hairstreaks with red cedar trees.

GRAY HAIRSTREAK
(S) Feb–Oct; (N) Apr–Oct

1–1¼in

Wings steel gray above, pale gray beneath. Red-orange and blue spots on hind wing above tail, like false head. Vertical line on undersides of wings is colored black, white and orange.

Caterpillar green, yellow or reddish with various markings and short yellow-brown hairs. Bores into flowers and fruits of many plants including cultivated beans, cotton and mallows.

Found in weedy disturbed areas, roadsides, vacant lots, open woods, fields and parks. Males perch on low shrubs and trees, flying out at other butterflies. Flight fast, erratic and close to the ground. Adults visit a wide variety of flowers for nectar, including winter cress, clovers and thistles.

Of the many Gray Hairstreaks in N. America, this is the most widespread. The others are mostly browner, lack the orange spot or the orange-bordered line on the underside.

Wings of male pale gray, of female black, both with many white spots giving them a checkered appearance. Blue hairs on body and wing bases. Underside of hind wings yellowish with bands of olive-green spots joined together.

Caterpillar pale yellow or brown with darker lines on back and sides, also white side lines and many white tubercles each with a single hair. Feeds on mallows, hibiscus and hollyhocks.

Found on highway verges, in back yards, vacant lots and parks as well as in river valleys, meadows and open woods. Males patrol their territories, flying regularly backwards and forwards or bask in the afternoon. Adults visit white-flowered fleabanes and asters, also beggars' ticks and clovers.

Several checkered skippers live in N. America, including three mountain species from the north and west, two desert species from the southwest and **Small Checkered Skipper**.

LARGE WHITE SKIPPER
(Calif.) most of year; (N) May–Sep   **1–1½in**

Wings of male creamy white with dark gray crescents forming borders and checkered fringes. Females have gray wing bases, a white central area and broadly checkered borders. Underside of hind wing pale brown and white.

Caterpillar pale yellow-green with numerous tubercles, each with white forked hair and several dark green and yellow lines. Feeds on globe mallows and hollyhocks.

Found in greener, often disturbed, parts of arid areas, in foothills, gullies, chaparral and near water. Flight swift and quite low to the ground. Males patrol in canyons searching for females and visit mud. Adults visit wild buckwheats and black sage, amongst other flowers, for nectar.

Other white skippers are much less common, being confined to extreme southern states. **Checkered Skippers** have white spots on gray or black wings.

CHECKERED WHITE
Spring, summer & fall

♀

♂

Wings white with checkered black markings, females with more black than males which may be almost all white in summer. Veins of undersides of hind wings have brown or olive scales.

Caterpillar striped blue-green and yellow with black spots. Feeds on members of mustard family including shepherd's purse, peppergrasses, winter cress, cultivated cabbages and turnips.

Found in lowland areas, from railroad yards and disturbed ground to fields, pastures and dunes. Males patrol in the afternoon in search of females, flight rapid and zigzagging or direct. Both sexes visit flowers of caterpillar host plants like winter cress and hedge mustard for nectar.

Western White: western mountains and lowland arctic areas.
Spring White: small, flies from February to May in western mountains and deserts.

Wings white, usually without a spot on fore wings. Undersides of hind wings creamy yellow with veins heavily covered with olive or brown scales. Some summer forms lack this veining.

Caterpillar green and velvety with yellow stripes on back and sides. Feeds on members of the mustard family including milkmaids, toothworts, water cress and winter cress.

Found in open deciduous woods and coniferous woods, especially where wet and on the tundra in the north. Absent from the southeast and southern Calif. Males patrol in daylight hours, flight relatively weak and slow, usually in woodland edges. Adults visit flowers of caterpillar host plants for nectar.

Cabbage White: black spots on fore wings and lacks heavy veins on undersides of hind wings.

Spring–fall

Wings white with black wing tips and black spots on fore wings, two in female, one in male. Underside of hind wing and underside of fore wing tip both yellow.

Caterpillar green with many fine hairs and yellow stripes on back and sides. A serious pest, feeds on cultivated cabbage plants, nasturtiums and other members of the mustard family.

Found in open areas but most commonly in cultivated fields and gardens of urban areas. Rare in extreme south and deserts. Males patrol in daylight. Flight lazy and wandering, one or two feet above the ground. Females may be seen fluttering about cabbage plants. Adults visit a wide variety of flowers.

No other white has the combination of yellow undersides to hind wings and black spots on fore wings.

PHOEBUS PARNASSIAN
Summer

2–3in

Antennae striped black and white. Wings of male white with black veins and spots, females grayer. Both sexes have red spots on hind wings and sometimes on fore wings.

Caterpillar black with row of yellow spots and many bristles. Feeds on stonecrops. Caterpillars take a year to complete development, overwintering when half grown.

Found in arctic tundra, mountain meadows and sagebrush, near to stonecrop plants, often high up in the mountains. Flies in colder weather than most butterflies. Males patrol during the day in search of females. Adults visit yellow flowers of daisy family for nectar.

Clodius Parnassian: found at lower elevations, antennae solid black, no red spots on fore wings.

OTHER WHITES

Pine White (1)
Wings white with black markings around wing tips. Found high up among the trees, in pine & fir forests from sea to mountains, B.C. to Calif. Caterpillars may be forest pest. Sometimes occur in huge numbers.

Western White (2)
Similar to Checkered White with black & white wings. Greenish scales on veins of undersides of hind wings. Western mountains & lowlands of far north, from Alaska to south Calif. & east to Manitoba.

West Virginia White (3)
Gray white with heavy gray-brown veins above & below. Moist mountain woods from the Great Lakes & Quebec to Georgia, especially where maples are present. Flies in spring, March–June, earliest in the south.

Great Southern White (4)
Large. White wings, fore wings tipped with black triangles. Females grayer than males. Beaches, islands, dunes & salt marshes in Florida & southern Texas, migrating north in summer up Mississippi & along Atlantic coast.

MARBLEWINGS & ORANGETIPS

Creamy Marblewing (1)
Wings creamy white with black or yellow-green marbling on fore wing tips & green marbling on undersides of hind wings. Coniferous forests, especially clearings & trails of Great Lakes region & western mountains.

Pearly Marblewing (2)
Small pearly white with black marbling at fore wing tips & green marbling on undersides of hind wings. Sagebrush, canyons & rocky areas in basins & foothills of western mountains. Flies in spring, April–May.

Sara Orangetip (3)
Male white, female white or yellow, both with bright orange black-rimmed tips on fore wings. Undersides of hind wings marbled in green. Western mountains, sunny woods & meadows, canyons & near the sea from Alaska to Calif.

Falcate Orangetip (4)
Wings white. Fore wings have black spots around rim & orange tips in male, not in female. Underside of hind wings marbled in greenish brown. Clearings, beside roads & streams in deciduous woods in eastern USA. April or May.

OTHER SULPHURS

Dogface Butterfly (1)
Unmistakable with its dogface design on fore wings. Color varies from yellow to pink. Open areas & open woods from southeastern USA, migrating in summer through midwest to northeast & Canada. Males gather at mud puddles.

Queen Alexandra's Sulphur (2)
Wings yellow with narrow black borders in males, little or no border in females. Meadows & roadsides in pine forests, & sage brush from western & central Canada to Nevada & New Mexico in the mountains.

Pink-edged Sulphur (3)
The most likely to be seen of several northern sulphurs, & distinctive with pink-fringed yellow wings. Open spaces, woods, meadows & roadsides across Canada & northern USA, south in mountains. Males gather at mud puddles.

Fairy Yellow (4)
Small, with light yellow wings & black wing tips. Underside of hind wings red-brown in winter forms, white in summer forms. Dry disturbed areas, coastal dunes & open pine woods in southeast USA.

FRITILLARIES

Fritillaries have orange wings with complicated black markings. The caterpillars feed mostly on violets. Large Fritillaries have silver spots on undersides of hind wings & are 2–4in across. Small Fritillaries are similar to large Fritillaries but most have red-brown undersides to hind wings instead of silver spots. They are mostly 1–1½in across. **Variegated Fritillary** has brown, orange & white undersides.

Variegated Fritillary (1)
Grasslands, roadsides, mountain meadows; resident in south, migrating north to Canada in summer.
Aphrodite (2)
Woods & meadows of Canadian, western & eastern mountains.
Zerene Fritillary (3)
Sunny meadows & openings in woods, roadsides, in western & northern mountains.
Titania's Fritillary (4)
Wet meadows, valleys, trails & clearings in mountains of west & east; northern tundra.

Mylitta Crescent (1)
Orange with crescentic patterns of black lines, black spots & a black border. Underside of hind wing has white crescents on margin. Woods, roadsides, vacant lots & meadows in lower mountains, B.C. to Calif. & New Mexico.

Bordered Patch (2)
Dark brown with very variable patterns of orange &/or white spots across wings. Underside of hind wing black with creamy bands & red spot at corner. Fields, woods, back yards, deserts, in southwest USA.

Northern Checkerspot (3)
Males bright yellow & orange, with color broken into network by brown lines; female usually darker. Open areas of forest in Rocky mountains & the Pacific states. Frequent puddle visitors.

Chalcedon Checkerspot (4)
Black or brown with bands of yellow &/or orange spots across all wings. Underside of wings has alternating bands of pale yellow & red. Open woods, roadsides, chaparral & deserts from Oregon to Arizona.

Yellowpatch Skipper (1)
Wings brown with orange patch
along top of fore wing.
Undersides of both wings have
yellow patches. Open grassy
areas, vacant lots, roadsides,
from southern Canada
throughout much of USA but
rare in south.

Uncas Skipper (2)
Wings orange-brown with
brown margins. Underside of
hind wings olive-brown with
white crescents & white-scaled
veins. Dry prairies & sage brush
from western Canadian prairie
provinces throughout midwest &
western USA.

Delaware Skipper (3)
Wings bright orange-yellow with
black borders on all four wings.
Undersides similar. Damp
fields, meadows & prairies as
well as roadsides & suburbs.
USA east of the Rockies.

Orange Giant Skipper (4)
Wings orange with black
markings. Undersides gray-
brown with orange band on fore
wing. Body furred with orange.
Mountains & mesas near agaves
in Arizona, Texas & New
Mexico.

116

OTHER SKIPPERS

Hoary Edge (1)
Wings triangular, dark brown with glassy yellow spots on fore wing & white edge to hind wing. Underside brown & black with white outer half to hind wing. Open woods, pastures, disturbed ground, usually with oak or pine. Eastern USA.

Golden Banded Skipper (2)
Wings dark brown with wide yellow band across each fore wing tip. Undersides brown with gray frosting & two bands of dark spots on hind wing. Moist woods & ravines. South & southeastern USA, north to New York State.

Small Checkered Skipper (3)
A tiny butterfly, little more than a half inch across. Brown with checkered white markings & white fringes. Underside of hind wings creamy white & brown. Prairies, grasslands & old fields, from Alberta south to New Mexico & Calif.

Southern Cloudywing (4)
Wings dark brown with white glassy spots in bands across fore wings; one spot hourglass-shaped. Undersides have varying shades of brown. Open areas from roadsides to grassland, barrens & powerline cuts. Eastern USA.

Shorttail Black Swallowtail (1)
Small black swallowtail with short tails & pale creamy yellow & blue spots. Mountains, canyons & deserts of western states. Males congregate at mud puddles.

Western Black Swallowtail (2)
Large black swallowtail with two rows of yellow spots in male, one marginal row in female. Orange spots on hind wing have "cross-eyed" black centers. Western USA from S. Dakota diagonally southwest to southern Calif. in arid areas.

Two-tailed Tiger Swallowtail (3)
Large yellow swallowtail with black-bordered wings, narrow vertical black stripes & two tails on each hind wing. Western USA from Dakotas & Oklahoma westward, in canyons, mountains & in city suburbs.

Pale Tiger Swallowtail (4)
Wings pale cream with black stripes & black borders. Long black tail on each hind wing. Dry mountain areas & canyons from B.C. to Calif. on both sides of the Rockies.

White M-Hairstreak (1)
Wings iridescent blue with dark margins, males brighter than females, with two tails on hind wing. Undersides gray with white line forming an "M" on hind wing. Southern USA from Iowa & Connecticut south, near oak trees usually in or near woods.

Colorado Hairstreak (2)
Deep purple wings with dark margins & red-orange spots near margins. Found in canyons & foothills of western & southwest USA near to Gambel oaks.

Great Blue Hairstreak (3)
Wings brilliant iridescent blue in males, duller in females & blue more restricted to base of wings; with one or two tails on hind wing. Underside purple-gray with blue-green spots over tail, forming false head. Southern USA from coast to coast near trees parasitized by mistletoe, usually in lowland areas.

119

OTHER BLUES

Western Pygmy Blue (1)
Tiny butterfly, only about a half inch across; wings mostly brown with blue bases, less blue in females. Underside of wings gray & brown with row of blue-centered black spots around rear margin of hind wing. Disturbed places, vacant lots & railroads in lowland & coastal areas in southwest & prairie states of USA. Caterpillars feed on pigweed, pickleweed & saltbush. Eastern Pygmy Blue browner, found in coastal areas of southeast.

Reakirt's Blue (2)
About one inch across, males have blue wings, females browner; both with black spots at rear of hind wing. Undersides of wings distinctive, brown & white with row of white-rimmed black spots on fore wing. Resident in southern states & migrate northwards each year, especially in the states adjoining the Mississippi. Most often found in arid areas & grassland. Caterpillars feed on legumes, including mesquite & indigos.

Arctic Blue (1)
About one inch across. Male has gray-blue wings, female brown, both with row of dots on rear of hind wing & small dark mark on each fore wing. Underside gray-brown with white spots. Lives in tundra of far north from Alaska to Labrador, also in Rocky Mountains & Black Hills, in forests, on slopes & mountain meadows. Caterpillars feed on alpine plants like saxifrages & androsaces.

Northern Blue (2)
About one inch across. Male has blue-purple wings, female brownish gray with orange spots around margins. Undersides light brown with thin black marginal line & row of blue, orange & black spots. Heathland & open areas in mountains & northern forests from B.C. to Labrador & in Rockies. Caterpillar feeds on crowberry, Hudson Bay tea & related plants. In some areas this butterfly is difficult to distinguish from Melissa Blue.

Index and check-list

All species in Roman type are illustrated
Keep a record of your sightings by checking the boxes